Sillage

The Fragrance that Lingers

An Anthology of
Prose and Poems by

Shrey Janardan

'Bazodumba'

Sillage
(n. French) The lingering trail of fragrance left in the air, after someone has passed by.

ISBN 979-8-89186-790-1

Second Edition

All original works by the author are available at
bazodumba.tumblr.com & www.youtube.com/@inexistence5760

Artworks by artist Gaurvi Sharma:
www.gaurvisharma.com **gaurvim**

Poem annotations provided by the author's parents.

All proceeds from this book shall go towards social causes espoused in memory of Shrey Janardan and Raza Nagpal.

In The Tapestry Of Time,
I Lingered Briefly,

A Fleeting Verse,
In Life's Grand Refrain.

Shrey Janardan

15.02.2005 – 07.06.2022

Dedication

Dear Son,

We can't believe that we won't see you again.

Your mom is shattered, your little sister is in disbelief and your dad is putting up a brave front, but deeply hurt inside.

Son, the beauty in the words you left behind, which speak about love, hope, despair and your zest for life, hold wisdom far beyond the 17 years of your brief stint here with us.

Today, these words are what comfort us the most.

You had once shared your aspiration of publishing your writings someday. With your permission, we would like to release your works to the world. Not just because we want your memory to live on, but because we believe the world deserves it.

Mumma, Papa
Feb 2024

Parents' Note
Reflections, Gratitude, and Infinite Love

Thank you for choosing to explore this book. Here, you'll find a collection of our son Shrey's musings, reflections and the profound lessons he left for all of us.

Shrey was born on 15th Feb 2005. Both my husband and I, serving air force officers at the time, were elated to welcome our charming bundle of joy. We lovingly nicknamed him Baby Shrey and he was so adorable and chubby that strangers would often request us for a photo with him!

As a baby, Shrey was remarkably naughty, his eyes always sparkling with mischievousness. On one occasion, he ingeniously polished our TV set with black shoe-polish, aiming to give it an extra shine! Another time, he cleverly used his dad's helmet as a convenient urinal, filling the inner sponge lining with 'holy water'. The uproarious look on his Dad's face, when he donned the helmet next day, remains a much etched hilarious memory ☺

Shrey was a free-spirited child, with an infectious and roaring laughter. He would light up every room he was in, delighting in the attention his playful antics would bring. In kindergarten, he was so fascinated by braids that he would perch behind the girls in the class and untangle their pleats, much to their annoyance. As parents, we had our hands full watching over him, making sure he was not in harm's way or that he was causing no harm!

As he grew, Shrey was drawn to reading and he admired warriors like Maharana Pratap and Karna. He had a fascination with soft toys, whom he fancied as his loyal soldiers. He would dress up as a warrior, and lead the soldiers to endless battles with gusto. He was never shy in doing this, even when he was twelve or thirteen. He was endlessly fascinated with Lego, Uno, and countless other games and could keep at them for hours, without a care in the world.

But, it was books that he loved most. Initiated early into literature by his father, he delved into mythology, Harry Potter, Sherlock Holmes and the works of Rick Riordan and John Green. Over time, his literary interests expanded to include diverse range of genres, from philosophy, fiction to classics and thrillers. He took great pride in his collection of books, and even started an online library for his school friends, when he was in his early teens.

As an armed forces family, we criss-crossed India, every few years. Despite the challenges of bidding farewell to friends and embracing new beginnings, Shrey never complained about the transfers. Each move introduced us to a diverse array of festivals and colors, and Shrey embraced the richness of these experiences. Whether it was Holi, Diwali, Ganesh Chaturthi, Christmas, Halloween, or Onam, he wholeheartedly enjoyed all celebrations. Chandigarh, with its stable five-year stint, held a special place in his heart, prompting him to declare it as 'Home' in one of his writings. It was during our time in Chandigarh that Shrey discovered his passion for writing, focusing much of his work on philosophy and mythology.

In July 2020, Shrey was in his eleventh class, when we were transferred to Bangalore. These were the times of the Covid -19 lockdown and Shrey struggled to acclimatise to his new surroundings and form new connections due to pandemic-related restrictions and quarantine measures. Turning to writing as a solace, his works from this period carry profound themes of philosophy, existentialism and loneliness. Shrey had a contemplative streak and he would often pen his thoughts during the quiet of late nights, sharing them as a blog on Tumblr or through video-posts on YouTube.

Some respite came, as online classes commenced. Interestingly, this period also signified a turning point in his life, as Shrey forged some of his most meaningful and profound friendships with buddies his age. His new friends were just as lively as him, sharing his interests in reading, contemplation, writing and late-night video game sessions!

Around this time, Shrey also met 'Starla', who was to be the love of his life. Shrey had excitedly shared details about her and she even visited our home a couple times for class notes etc. Over time, Shrey and Starla developed a profound connection that went way beyond ordinary teenage romance. Theirs was a deep, soulful companionship, where they bonded as much over deep philosophical quests as nuances of everyday living, eventually becoming each other's unwavering pillars of support.

Shrey was also exceptionally bright, although academic excellence didn't particularly concern him. Despite minimal study time, he achieved good grades in his tenth and eleventh classes. For him, education was a means to explore his interests, particularly in English literature and management studies. Always vibrant, he attended parties even during the twelfth board exam season. By May 2022, he had secured admission to Jindal Global University near Delhi, and his twelfth board exams were going exceptionally well due to the hard work he had invested in the preceding months.

But then, the last day of his twelfth-grade exams, turned out also to be Shrey's last day with us. The night before, he went to bed filled with excitement, pleased that his exams were progressing well and anticipating a well-deserved break the next day with his friends. Plans for a post-exam celebration were in place. We had retired early that night and around 10:30pm Shrey came to our room, rummaging for his laptop to pack it for the next day's gaming session.

On his way out he bade us goodnight.

That was the last we saw of him.

Shrey didn't wake up the next morning, passing away quietly in his sleep.

It was a parents' worst nightmare come true. There was no prior illness or health warnings, no goodbyes, no farewells, no time for hugs – one moment he was there, and the next, he was not.

He had departed suddenly and unceremoniously, leaving behind a 'future that never was,' as he had expressed in one of his writings.

The subsequent autopsy report was inconclusive but revealed an unusual enlargement of Shrey's heart (cardiomyopathy) with tiny blood clots. Could this have been a consequence of a Covid infection he had contracted six months prior, or perhaps a reaction to the Covid vaccine he was administered a month before his passing? Unfortunately, these questions remain without clear answers, and our search for understanding seems to have reached an impasse. Accepting this reality is a challenging aspect of life — one that we find difficult to reconcile.

The notion that things might have unfolded differently, if there was even a slight cautionary sign related to his health, is a poignant source of pain. Should we have conducted precautionary cardiac tests post-COVID? It's a question without a definitive answer and a regret that we will take to our graves.

The grief we've experienced has taught us to value the good things in life, even amidst all of life's hardships. It led us also to explore Shrey's writings with greater depth, uncovering the layers of meaning within. As his verses unfolded, we came to view our son as an unlikely teenage philosopher, unraveling the mysteries of life, love, and death. In 'Purpose', his verses capture the essence of pure Love:

> 'The world may be a stage,
> And I may be a performer on the said stage;
> But my eyes always look for you in the audience,
> It is for you that I give the performance.'

In 'Sand Castles in the Air', his verses comment on the hollowness of pursuing hedonistic materialism (building sand castles) in one's life:

> *'Building Sand Castles in the Air*
> *Is but a waste of time.*
> *And time withers away,*
> *Like the leaves in Autumn.'*

Shrey's vivid portrayal of the inevitability of death and its dark beauty has the power to stun and mesmerize any reader. How could a lively, vivacious teenager, who never in his life had a run-in with death, pen lines like those he did in 'Sillage'. Could it be that his higher consciousness had the premonition of the impending exit?

> *'You'll try to evade the sly smile of Death as long as you can*
> *but the sad truth is that you must, one day, give it a caress,*
> *for all that was born must one day cross the waters of Styx*
> *on a boat with the ferryman'.*

> *'We're all damned souls, living a lie, waiting for the truth*
> *to catch up and when it does, you leave this world,*
> *empty-handed, just the way you came, but you leave a lot*
> *to the world, to those who loved you and to those you loved.*
> *You leave them memories and possessions, but most impor*
> *tantly, you leave them your Sillage (lingering fragrance)'.*

In 'Reaper,' love and death find themselves intertwined as he implores fate to claim his life instead of his lover's, only to discover that fate had already sealed a bargain – his lover sacrificing her life for his!

In 'A Second Chance,' Shrey's enthusiastic celebration of life is revealed as he awakens in a surreal realm and encounters God directly. Reflecting openly on the intricacies of human existence ("it wasn't the best existence, but it was perfect nevertheless"), Shrey declines God's extraordinary offer to exchange roles. Instead, he expresses a desire for a second chance at life, emphasizing the profound beauty he perceives in the imperfect yet perfect nature of human existence.

In 'Optimistic Nihilism', written as part of a school essay, Shrey acknowledges the apparent lack of inherent meaning in the universe but encourages people should embrace life with a positive outlook and create one's own meaning and purpose.

> *'It took me a long time to realise that no one else*
> *is going to help me find meaning in life. I realized*
> *that it is my life, and it's meaning is mine to make'*

> *'I strongly believe that nothing we do actually*
> *matters, but I find peace in it.'*

> *'For me, optimistic nihilism is what differentiates*
> *living from existing'.*

Shrey's writings exhibit a deep reverence for life, portraying it genuinely as fleeting, mortal, and marked by both peaks and valleys. It is as if the boy had accessed a wellspring of boundless otherworldly wisdom.

Today, these writings bring us peace and a sense of restoration. Probably, he knew it was meant to be like this.

We invite the reader to embrace the 'Sillage' of our beloved child, urging you to explore the essence embedded in these writings. We hope that these works not only inspire but also stir you to contemplate more deeply about your own legacy and the Sillage you wish to leave behind.

Bijoy and Mandeep
Parents of Shrey Janardan. Feb 2024.

Contents

Amor

LOVE'S EMBRACE

umbrella

Her

The Moon resides in her eyes,
Entire constellations in her smile,
The Sun in her warmth
And home in her scent.

There's pearls in her tears,
Hope in her laugh,
Love in her words,
And a silvery shimmer on her face.

The Sirens envy her voice,
Her beauty makes Venus blush.
She's smarter than Athena,
And fiercer than Bellona.

She's the sound of silence,
The raindrops falling to the ground,
The rustling of pages,
And all the good there ever was.

Sep 2, 2021
#Love #Love Poem #Couple #Books&Libraries #Quotes #Poems
#Romantic #Romanticpoem

Infinity

In my head, when I look,
at the grandest canvas possible;
I see that life, the world around us,
everything that we know and do not know;
It's all meaningless.

It's all going to end in oblivion.
It's all going to stop existing after a while.
It's all one big *Nullity*.

And then I look at you,
and all I see is *Infinity*.

Aug 23, 2021
#Forever #ForeverLove #Love #Writing #Infinity

Parents' Note: These verses are a heartfelt dedication to 'Starla,' the radiant light in Shrey's life. She entered Shrey's world around the time he moved from Chandigarh to Bangalore, during the Covid lockdown of 2020. Whether by fate or chance, Shrey and Starla developed a profound connection that far surpassed ordinary teenage affections. They shared aspirations, delved into the mysteries of life, and stood as unwavering pillars of support for each other from the moment they met until Shrey's passing in June 2022. The name 'Starla,' as chosen by Shrey in his writings, is retained here to respect her privacy.

We

Let's build a house
On the moon
With a fireplace
And three bedrooms

And an attic
For all your art
And so much love
That it fills our hearts.

I won't need oxygen
I'll be happy with you
We'll live a life together
With people few

Let's build a house
On the moon
With a fireplace
And three bedrooms.

Dec 11, 2021
#Poem #Home #Love#Moon
#HomeOnTheMoon #Dreams #Goals

Purpose

I know we're not going to be known to the world
because of our love,
That our love won't ever leave
an imprint in history,
Or the fate of humanity in general;
But in every love story,
The author writes about people like you and me.

In every thing of beauty,
It is your face and my love for you that I see.
I love you like the hot, dry sand of the desert loves
the cold, wet droplets of water
That falls on it when it rains.

The world may be a stage,
And I may be a performer on the said stage;
But my eyes always look for you in the audience,
It is for you that I give the performance.

I exist, only for you,
That, I feel, is my purpose
On this planet full of crowds.

It is in these crowds that I see how different you are,
For in my eyes, you glow, you're perfect.
Not dissimilar to a goddess of the night;
For in crowds, I see not people, just you.
I love you; you have given meaning to my life.

Aug 15, 2021
#Love #Insignificance #Happiness #Couple #Romantic

You and Me

Perhaps it was an accident,
That you came into my life.

Perhaps it was my luck,
That you were just the girl for me.

Perhaps it was coincidence,
That we simply were, here and now.

But perhaps it was fate's hand all along,
Nudging and pointing.

You to Me,
And Me to You.

Apr 22, 2022

In Love

The slightest assurance
That you're doing okay
That you're living and not merely existing
Is enough to make me travel
Through the worlds that I'm stuck between.

The mere fact that you're in my life
Adds colour to my otherwise grey journey
Through time and space.

The mere fact that you are,
Is enough to make me
The luckiest man on earth.

Every time I make you smile,
I'm living life, moment by moment.

Every time you cry,
I have to be the one to make you smile,
To make you laugh,
Because even one tear coming out of your eyes
Causes me pain beyond measure.

Which I guess is fair,
Because my love for you cannot be
measured either.

I love you.

Aug 16, 2021
#Inlove #Love #Romantic #Couple #HappyEverAfter

Us

And when I look at the lines on my hand,

It is your name that I see,

Written a thousand times in gold.

 Aug 30, 2021
#Love #LoveQuotes #LoveAestheticQuotes #Aesthetic
#Couple#Romantic #RomanticQuotes

Starla

It wasn't the first time he found himself thinking of Starla.
She'd left a long time ago,
So many years had slipped by, he had lost count.

It's not as if he had not moved on
Sure, it had hurt like hell, but
He too had gone on with his life,
  Fallen in love again, and flown in time.

        But in times like these,
            When he was all alone in his bedroom, crying on the
              floor,
                When his wife was at work and his baby girl
                  asleep,
                  He'd think of her.

                  The first who broke his feeble heart,
                  The first hand he ever held,
                  The first love he ever trusted.

                  He wipes his tears as he hears his daughter
                  stir in her sleep,
                  Having a nightmare, maybe.
                  He goes to her and says,
                'Calm down, Starla. I'm here, you're okay.'

            And perhaps he only ever trusted her.
            Perhaps he still did.
          In his little black diary,
        The one where he wrote his poems and sonnets,
      She was there.
    In a way, she had never left, had she?

Apr 14, 2022

Before
You Leave

Before you leave,
I ask for these kisses three.

A kiss to remember you,
Your loving and perfect smile.

A kiss to celebrate us,
Our love short and sweet.

O you may go now,
Just give me one last kiss,
For you to fall in love with me again.

Dec 19, 2021

#Love #Kiss #Books&libraries #Quotes #Relationship #Couple #Poem #Sad

Parent's Note: This poem beautifully captures the yin-yang of love and loss. As he wrote to Starla, "You knit your soul into me, I will knit you into a poem"

Eternal Love

"I love you. I always will", he'd say to her whenever she was
distressed.

Little did he know that it wasn't the always that soothed her.
It never had been.

Nor was it anything else that he would say, that had mattered.
What really soothed those waves of panic and tremors of fear was
- just him.

The way his lips moved when he spoke, the way he talked in what
could only have been a soft whisper,

And of course, the way his lips would touch his teeth, much like
the way he touched her heart.

He could have said anything in that moment, in the same
exact way, and she wouldn't have reacted one bit differently.

She knew she was safe.

The sound of his voice and his hand caressing her head, it meant
the world to her,

Not just the world, it was home.

As he wipes her tears with his gentle fingers, she lets out a smile
and says

"Ditto"

Apr 8, 2022
#Love #Care #Safespace #Comfort #Home

A Life Together

I wanna wake up with you every morning
for the rest of my life.

Sep 1, 2021

#Love #Loveaesthetic #Aesthetic
#Quote #Lovequotes

Saudade

THE YEARNING

Cloudburst

The rustling leaves of the Fall,
Flying with the wind,
An unbearable ache,
For the departed downpour.

The coldness of the Winter,
Harsh as the truth,
A frostbitten feeling,
And a deluge inside.

The regenerating Spring,
Grass greener than ever,
New buds sprouting,
And making headways.

The scorch of the Summer,
Sweltering in solitude,
The mornings un-misting,
As vehemence faded.

But behold a drizzle,
Welcomed as ever,
Petrichor[1] emanating,
Cloudburst soon to come.

Parent's Note: Shrey left us a few months after he wrote this, right before the monsoon rains. We are left to wonder what he had in mind when he wrote the last line about "Cloudburst soon to come"?

[1] The pleasant smell of dry mud soaking i the water, accompanying the first rain after a dry hot summer.

Way Too Long

It's been Way Too Long,
Since I last saw you.

They say that with enough creativity,
One can imagine other people's voices in one's head.

And it breaks my heart to say this, but your voice
I may soon forget what it sounds like.

And it will be tucked away,
In the corners of my mind.
Right next to your widest smile,
And your loudest laugh.

Dec 11, 2021
#Missing you #Missing #Imagine #VoicesInTheHead #Love
#Separation #Alone #Loneliness #Lonely

Parent's Note: These verses resonate deeply in the wake of Shrey's departure. It has been a year since Shrey left us, and his memories remain vivid, providing solace. Yet, we can't help but worry if, with time, these cherished memories might slowly fade and retreat into the recesses of our aging minds. Each day, it feels as if Shrey's scent is drifting farther away from our recollections. If only there were technological means to preserve his scent, keeping it with us eternally!

Memories

Memories.

They're the reminders of a forgotten and perhaps, forgiven past.
And sometimes, it feels as if these memories are a curse.

They remind me of the things I once did, believing that
I was the king of the universe, when
[in reality] I was bound by the chains of my own genius.

Alas, I failed to see them for what they were,
A thousand arrows.

Being rubbed against a whetstone, becoming
Sharper with each passing day,
That will one day attack me together and
Make me bleed to death.

Oct 30, 2021
#Memories #Painfulmemories #Books&Libraries #Quotes
#Writing #Bittersweet

Parent's Note: In 2021, post the Covid lockdown, Shrey made a slew of strong friendships both in the real and the online world. However, his writings from that period also unveil a concealed pain and yearning, powerful emotions surfacing from the depths within. In hindsight, it seems as if he's communicating from another world, pondering unfulfilled dreams and the incomplete canvas of his life.

Missing You

When I go through old photographs and videos,
it feels as if I've opened a rusty trunk full of
memories out of which come a thousand shards
of the glass that used to be a happier past.

That's the thing about the past, isn't it? You can
try and hold on to it but eventually it fades away.
You start losing the whole picture. The glass
breaks. It always does. And you can do nothing
about it. With time, you forget those memories
but they're still there, somewhere.

And someday, something small and insignificant
will remind you of that glorious past, of those
joyful memories and you will smile and be
unsettled for a while and then you will continue
what you were doing as if nothing had happened.

As if you never tasted that bittersweet memory
again. You will never be there again and you will
pretend that you never were.

Parents' Note: This poem speaks to us directly, capturing the
constant ache as we miss our son every moment of our lives. The
hurt is immense, as one comes to terms with the fact that there is no
way to start afresh, fix things, rewind time or bring back our departed
loved one. Even as we remember and cherish the happy times we all
spent together as a family, it is hard to accept that there won't be any
'new moments' to enjoy together, only 'old memories' to reminisce.

Dec 11, 2021
#Missing #DoYouMissMeLikeImissYou? #MissYou #MissingYou #Past
#Memories #MovingOn

Late

He'd stare at her a second too long,
Smiling his bittersweet smile,
A thousand things to say,
But none escaped his soft lips.

Alas, when his lips parted to say,
The words that long needed saying,
She was long gone.

And then he wept,
Oh, he wept, he wept, he wept.

Apr 23, 2022
#Troy #Trojanhorse #Betrayal #Hurt #Achilles #Iliad #Bittersweet

Parent's Note: In actuality, it was Shrey who departed from the world abruptly, without a farewell for Starla or any of his loved ones.

Unreal

It feels as if my whole past was one big dream,
and everything I've ever done wasn't real.

Or if it was, then I didn't do it.
It was just luck or something.

And now, I feel like it is time to wake up.
The dream is ending... or maybe it has
already ended.

I do not know anymore. I feel like it's time
to come back to Reality but how do I do that without
knowing what's real and what's not?

The blows of reality are breaking the mirror
of the dream and I am in between worlds.

I'm confused. And scared. And helpless.

And the worst part is that there's no one there to hold
my hand and tell me that it's all going to be okay.

Dec 11, 2021

Saudade

Conversations forgotten,
A world beyond.
A trap in time,
A future that never was.

The sentence incomplete,
My late lament.
Begone, O' ache,
The rain is long gone.

Mar 11, 2022

Parents' Note: Saudade was a word Shrey loved. It's a Portuguese word which denotes the feeling of deep longing or sadness for a loved one, who isn't there anymore. It's a special feeling that holds both the sadness of loss and the warmth of what was. Shrey wrote this piece three months before his demise. One wonders also whether references to 'a world beyond,' 'a future that never was,' and 'the sentence incomplete' came from an intuition that the time to 'move on' was around the corner?

Shrey used to have Saudade as his WhatsApp status for a while. His mom would ask him, "What is the longing for, son?" In response, he'd elusively feign ignorance. At first, his mom didn't know what Saudade meant or felt like.

Now, with Shrey's passing, we feel Saudade in our bones, every moment of our lives.

The Tempest Dance

PANIC, FEAR, DESPAIR, HOPE

The Reaper

"Reaper, O' Reaper[2]
I implore you, do not take her.

She is the sunlight,
And the spark that ignites.
She's as soft as cotton,
And as bright as the dawn.
She's as sweet as honey,
And means the world to me.

Reaper, O' Reaper,
Take me instead of her."

"Oh Earthling,
Tell me what I should do,
For she asked the same of me last night,
When I came to reap your soul."

Sep 26, 2021
#Love #Death #WouldYouDieForMe
#DieForAnother #DieForLove
#Reaper

[2] The Grim Reaper - embodiment of
   death, reaper of souls

34

Storms of Panic

The wall of denial is crumbling down
The waves of panic are crashing
On the shores of my mind.

The future is now
This moment is nothing but pain.

I wish to be in a state of *inexistence*
But that is an irreversible process
Which is why I cannot undergo it.

I am not wallowing in self-pity
I am looking for hope, when there is none
For I can't see the light beyond the tunnel.

Storms of panic won't last
Storms always cease.

The future is always to come
And what has come will pass.

Wishing to be damned
Is not a trait of the damned,
For they long for naught.

Hope may be silent,
Hoping for hope may seem fraught,
But that's what life is about.

And tunnels curve.

Make pathways like a river and flow along
Or crash through and seize hope yourself.

Aug 30, 2021
#Panic #Poem #Existential crisis #Fear

Parents' Note: The theme of inexistence echoes through several of Shrey's writings and YouTube videos. He describes it as an 'in-between world,' where perfection and unreality coexist. In these works, he yearns to re-join the real world, embracing all its imperfections. Readers can explore Shrey's YouTube series on this theme, which features his own voice, at https://www.youtube.com/@inexistence5760

Melancholy

O' ethereal monster
Tell me why I feel,
This melancholy of sorts.

Why I despise
The line undeviating,
The leaves shedding,
And the wind rustling.

Tell me what I fear more,
The end of the summer
Or the oncoming fall?

Nov 27, 2021

Stardust

"We were born of stars and in death we will return to them.
Let's not strive to be blackholes in the meantime.
Let's illuminate the world instead of darkening it,
Let's prove we are worthy of being stardust."

- 'Arrow of Entropy' by Courney M. Privett

It is as if I have both a black hole and a white hole within me
Whatever one emits, the other swallows
Keeping me at an equilibrium.

But sometimes,
The quantity one emits
Differs from what the other can accept
Disrupting my equilibrium.

Sometimes I wish
I didn't need an equilibrium.

Sometimes I wish
I were less than who I am, and
Sometimes, just sometimes
I wish I never were.

Dec 10, 2021.

Fear

Joy, laughter, wonder, hope.
That's all we live for, don't we?

Yet, we also live for fear
Because there's nothing as beautiful as the face of fear itself.

How so, you ask?

Just the adrenaline rushing through your veins
Just your heart pacing as fast as it can
Just the face of death lurking somewhere behind you.

A billion reasons to be paralysed in fear,
But you're running.

Facing fear and running from it,
Are two different choices
That are way too similar.

Fear, in its essence, is rational.

Dec 11, 2021

The Dark

*"And if you hurt me, well that's okay, baby.
Only words bleed inside these pages, you just hold me
And I won't ever let you go"*

-'Photograph' by Ed Sheeran

The words ring in his ears in a unique and unforgivable way.
This used to be our song, a voice in his head said.

Alas, August is but a distant memory, lost in a vast ocean of time,
Hidden somewhere just out reach.

The songs of birds and the chirping of crickets,
And the magic in the wind is long gone.
And what's left is the cold month of December,
Etching its way into a new beginning into a new year.

But is it really another beginning?
Another chance at being someone else?
Or is it just a sum of all his mistakes from the past
Integrating into his future?

The lies of Father time are now completely see-through,
More transparent than air itself.

He's been looking for hope for a long time now,
But tonight is the longest night of the year.
And the one he dreads the most,
Because he knows that he's afraid of the dark,
And of being alone.

What his heart truly desires though,
Is for someone to hold his hand
Through the darkness and into the bright golden Summer.

The fall has been tough, but the Winter will be tougher
And his journey isn't even close to being over yet.
He doesn't know what's next,
The songbird's wallow or the wolf's howl[3]
But he knows there's only one way to find out...

Jan 3, 2022

Parents' Note: This poem weaves a tapestry of dual narratives. On one level, it mirrors the uncertainties of earthly existence, the transition from one year to the next with fresh aspirations. Simultaneously, it delves into a spiritual dimension, where December marks the culmination of one life, and the new year signifies rebirth. The mist-covered woods in the original setting further hints at this transcendence. The anticipation of what lies ahead in this new beginning, whether in the earthly or spiritual sense, remains unknown until experienced. Additionally, the reference to Father Time adds a layer of symbolism, representing both the relentless march of time and the judgment of one's deeds. It eerily aligns with Shrey's fate, devoured by Father Time at a tender age.

[3] Unrestrained, happy singing of a bird or a wolf's howl (indicative of imminent death).

Straw to the Drowning Man

Honestly, every time I feel like
I've had enough of this cruel life,
It gives me something to hold on to.

One little moment, one little thing.
And I find myself holding on to it as tightly as I can.

Because at the end of the day,
I don't wish to die.
I just wish to stop living the way I am
and I'll cling on to the tiniest thing that gives me hope,
however small it may be.

Nov 21, 2021
#Hopelessness #Life #Books&Libraries #Quotes
#HoldingOn #HoldingOnToHope #HoldingOn

Parents' Note: Shrey wrote this poignant piece during a rather intense phase of heart-break. It is however tragically ironic that just as he overcame all transient challenges, the loneliness of the lockdown and was poised for much success in life, the curtains were drawn rather abruptly in his sleep. His life remains an enigma to us, especially with these otherworldly writings. The question lingers – was it all guided by cosmic order, or merely a sequence of random events?

Bittersweet

Painful, bittersweet memories
From a long forgotten past,
Whose ghost still remains to this day.

Lingering at the brink of my consciousness,
Urging me to move forward
When everything else says I shouldn't.

A false ray of sunlight
Which promises to brighten my day,
But ends up making
The darkness even more prominent.

Feb 14, 2022
#Bittersweet #Memories #Writing

Despair

Lost in a city of lies,
With no one to turn to and no place to call home.

A warrior without a cause,
A god without religion.

Stretched beyond my breaking point,
Even hope has given up on me.

Soulless and alone, I don't think,
I have it in me to take another step again.

Aimlessly wandering, a hollow existence,
Thoughts floating, mind sinking.

That is who I am now,
And that is who I will be.

Dec 14, 2021
#Lost #Hopeless #Emo #Alone #Loneliness #books & libraries #quotes

Breached Walls

The ghost of a memory,
A dying wish,
And haunting screams,
Echo through my walls.

O' my walls,
My walls so high,
Why'd you bend low
For the Trojan Horse's neigh?

Mar 24, 2022

#Troy #Trojanhorse #Betrayal #Hurt #Achilles #Iliad #Bittersweet

Parents' Note: Can death come uninvited, if one just wrote about it? Even if one was a healthy 17-year-old boy? Why did you bend low for the 'Trojan horse' of death to enter? Why, our son, why?

Timelessness

INFINITY & BEYOND

Knowledge

Sometimes I lie awake at night,
wondering what it would feel like,
to be bound by the chains of Father Time.

Of course, lying awake is just a figure of
speech for I simply drift in this cosmos,
and all others, beyond time.

I'm simply there, without being there.

I've lived a million lives, yet not once have I been alive.
I've seen a billion dreams, a billion hopes,
burn to ashes and outshine the Sun.

I've seen it all. And that too in less than an instant and in more
than an eternity, depending on who you ask.

Ever wondered what it'd feel like to know
everything there is to know,
Yet not be able to speak it?

Ever wondered what it'd be like, if you had no concept of time?
Chaos ensues, yet there is order in it,
For even seemingly random events, can be predicted,
given enough data.

Of course, I've got no memory, I simply exist
In all of time and space as one unchanging unit.

Without a clue as to who or what I am,
Every instant that passes, I perceive it,
yet I can't hold on to it.

Time, my friend, is a funny thing.
And indeed, so am I.

May 9, 2022

Parents' Note : This composition seems to offer an intriguing glimpse into life and the afterlife. The phrase 'less than an instant or more than an eternity' hints at time running at different pace in different planes of existence. The expression 'perceiving everything but being unable to hold on to it' hints at a premonition of the imminent tragedy. What interpretation, apart from that of soul rebirth and memories from past lives, can we derive from this passage? Were these the musings of a prophetic subconscious or reflections guided by an otherworldly force?

Gods

An alternate universe probably exists where Man
did not eat the forbidden fruit,
Where he lies happy!
Naked and blissfully oblivious to the
imperfections of the Universe,
Because he's stuck in Eden, a perfect world.

We, however, live in a world where Man,
Was curious enough to eat the apple.
Man's curiosity is what led him,
To make the choice to become a god.

We live in a world where Man creates and Man destroys,
To raise or to raze, Man makes the choice.

We, fellow humans, are our own gods.

We're free in the true sense merely
because we were curious enough,
To commit the first sin.
That led to Man being expelled from a perfect,
Yet hollow world into an imperfect but real world.
Look around, humans!

Mankind has made this world a perfect one.
With love and happiness and hate and suffering.

We. Are. Gods.

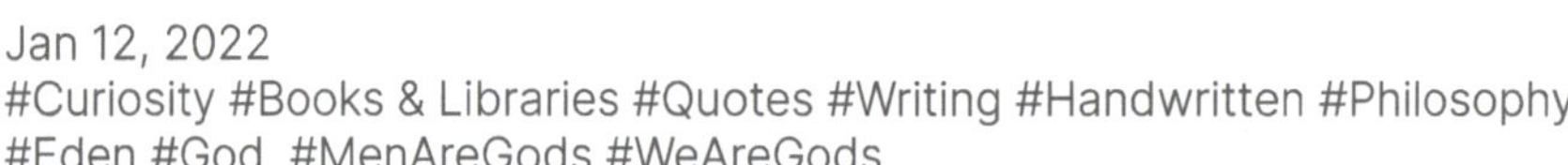

Jan 12, 2022
#Curiosity #Books & Libraries #Quotes #Writing #Handwritten #Philosophy
#Eden #God #MenAreGods #WeAreGods

A Letter to
the Beyond

There will come a day, long after we're dust,
When the entire universe as we know it, shall collapse on itself.

A forever expanding infinity that became so big, it ate itself up,
Killing not only entire civilisations, their history, culture, but also
time itself.

There shall remain no Sun, nor a shred of evidence that we ever were,
if at all.

Time will end, only to begin again, if only to forge a better world.

But, just in case this piece of paper survives the literal end of time.
[And I know, it won't]

"We were here before you.
In a time parallel to yours, one unknown to you.
We had spread far and wide and were called the human race.
Who we were, does not matter anymore, though.
We made our mistakes, it's time for you to make yours.
Your time, too, shall runout someday.
Make every moment count.
Godspeed!"

The Essence of Being

LIFE'S BOUNDLESS JOURNEY

Sand Castles in the Air

There exists a road,
A road with turns every now and then.
It bends, it curves, it never ends.
It's a path one must follow
Because it's forbidden to halt.

All that keeps one going,
Are Castles.
But one would be foolish to think,
That these Castles aren't made of sand.
These Sand Castles in the Air,
Are perfect and pretty,
But alas, they're too good,
To ever be true.

But that's all one can have,
In this road full of travellers;
Travellers that misspeak and hurt,
But also travellers that love.

Building Sand Castles in the Air
Is but a waste of time.
And time withers away,
Like the leaves in Autumn.

Like a Perthro[4] one must wait,
To be filled.
But all one ever knew,
Was to build Sand Castles in the Air.

Sep 2, 2021

These verses reflect on the hollowness of pursuing materialistic pleasures in life, symbolized by the act of building sand castles. Shrey drew inspiration for this poem from a casual conversation with his love that included a mention of the phrase 'sand castle'. This idea lingered in his thoughts and he evolved it into a beautiful poem about the transient essence of existence.

[4] Pertho is an alphabet of the old writing system and represents fate or luck.

#Melancholy #ExistentialNihilism #Insignificant #Sky
#Philosophy #Books&Libraries #Quotes #Writing

What if?

What if life were an endless ocean
Where it's only land I yearn.

It's full of peace and calm
Right before the storm.

Sometimes you swim
Sometimes you give in.

Maybe you want to sink
You want to do it in a blink.

It isn't easy, swimming.
It's tougher than falling.

And in this ocean you are born.
But like the light bearer[5] you're thrown
In another's sea.
Where everything you be[6]...

[5] The light bearer here refers to Lucifer or morning star, who while aspiring for
a higher seat in heaven, was cast down to the underworld.

[6] The poem ends abruptly, much like Shrey's life did.

Why me?

Why me? Said I
Under the bridge as the sky filled,
With the seemingly perfect blend
Of red, pink blue and orange from the setting Sun.

The same Sun that has made
the miracle of life possible
On this small speck of order
In the vast multitudes of chaos
that is the world we live in.

And yet it is the same Sun
that will one day expand
Into something so big
that it will scorch the Earth
and all the life on it.

And here I am!
asking why I,
of all people, had to be.

Questioning Life

A world or a snow globe
What do I live in?

Or are they the same?

Moments in eternity
Or eternities in moments?

April 1, 2022
#Snowglobes #Winter #Snow #QuestioningLife #aesthetic

Parents' Note : The phrase 'Moments in Eternity' or 'Eternity in Moments' signifies that certain moments hold a timeless significance, transcending the constraints of linear time.

Musings

REFLECTIONS IN VERSE

Meaning

We, humans are so naïve and ignorant.

Man's search for meaning began long ago and it started with the assumption that there was meaning in life, to begin with.

We've looked far beyond the point where the skies end and we've looked far beyond the depths of the deepest sea and all that was found was evidence pointing to how alone and insignificant we truly are.

It does not matter what we do with our lives, for no matter what choices one makes, it is still not going to affect the end of the world. The Sun will die, the Earth will perish someday; and there's no preventing that.

The universe, which is forever expanding, has made it clear that entropy is going to get us all in the end;[7] and there's nothing we can do about it.

Then why, you ask, is Man looking for meaning?

The answer to that question is not one that most people understand. The thing is, in the great scheme of things, nothing really matters but we don't exactly live in the great scheme of things, do we?

We're all really just existing in our own worlds. So even though nothing really matters, it doesn't matter that it doesn't matter.

There is no one universal meaning to life that applies to every living being on this planet, because every individual is unique and special, and something as important as meaning or purpose in life cannot be generic.

Meaning is something a person has to find out for himself.

We've been looking out at the stars with a telescope for so long that we've forgotten to appreciate the beauty in what we have on this round lump of mud we call home.

Meaning isn't in big perfect things like the Moon or the Sun, it is in the small imperfections like the way the wind blows on a cold day or the way flowers wither away in the Autumn.

We don't live in a perfect world, and that is precisely what makes it perfect.

Sep 7, 2021
#Meaning Of Life #Meaning #Humanity #Humanity #Nihilism #ExistentialNihilism #Optimistic Nihilism #Books&Libraries #Quotes #Philosophy #Writing

[7] Heat death of the Universe" hypothesis

Sillage

Sillage

Death is an upheaval with a pretty face.

It comes without apprising; no harbinger to alert you of its arrival; and it steals the invaluable: life.

You spend your whole life ignoring your impending doom, living in denial until one day, the ruthless angel of death reaps your soul and departs and leaves your loved ones in pieces.

Someday, you will be gone, but there were those before you and there will be those after you. The Universe, alas, does not revolve around you.

You'll try to evade the sly smile of Death as long as you can, but the sad truth is that, you must, one day give it a caress, for all that was born must one day cross the waters of Styx on a boat with the ferryman.

We're all damned souls, living a lie, waiting for the truth to catch up and when it does, you leave this world, empty-handed, just the way you came.

But you leave a lot to the world, to those who loved you and to those you loved. You leave them memories and possessions, but most importantly, you leave them your **Sillage**.

Nov 27, 2021
#Sillage #Hope #Death #Charon #Greek mythology #Philosophy
#Beyond death

Parents' Note:

Metaphorically, Sillage refers to the lingering memory or essence one leaves behind, much like the enduring fragrance of a perfume in the air.

This excerpt from Shrey's writings is amongst his most profound works. His ability to delve into life's realities, particularly death and its aftermath, remains a mystery to us. Even after discussing this brilliant piece with him, we only fully comprehended its truth in the wake of his passing. The poignant experiences of losing him, witnessing the unused remnants of his possessions and yearning for his physical presence emphasize the absolute truth in his words.

How did our lively, literature-loving son ever gain such profound insights into life and death? Was it from the books he read, or was there something more, something otherworldly guiding him? Were these writings his way of calming his restless soul, foretelling a truth that he had sensed?

The answers remain elusive. Only one thing is certain: he's no longer here to share with us any more of his wisdom and literary brilliance.

Fragments of Good

Humans are such fragile creatures.

One moment they're there, and in another, they're not. They're stuck in a circle that has neither beginning nor end.

The world they live in is barely there, yet there is nothing more real than it.

All that is born must one day die, and so, these fragile pieces of glass must one day break for they have committed the sin of being born and they shall pay the price by being rewarded by life, only for it to be taken away, without any forewarning.

Chaos is the norm and existence is the anomaly.

Chaos rules, but there's order in small pockets of this world.

There are fragments of good: joy, wonder, laughter, hope, kindness, sacrifice, candour, bravery and most importantly, love.

Love and death are the two most beautiful things these fragile beings experience and they add all the colour one needs to fill their empty canvas.

The threat of one's impending doom is enough to make existence bearable.

Imagine living forever.

What a pitiable existence it would be, to try everything and grow tired of it. To enjoy all this world has to offer, only to see it die with one's own eyes.

What joy can one find when they have seen all the fragments of good this barely existent world has to offer?

Humans live, but they all must, one day, die.

They live, they laugh, they love and they die. And that's beautiful.

One shouldn't seek immortality not because it is impossible to achieve but because it is an existence no one deserves to go through.

Imagine the pain of loving all the good this fragile world has to offer and then see it perish one day, whilst the immortal stares at it from a distance, helpless.

The fragility of the human condition is what gives existence itself a purpose and meaning.

To love is beautiful, but to die, is even more so.

Sep 5, 2021
#BeautyInDeath #Beauty In Death #Books&Libraries #Quotes #Writing #Philosophy #Death #Beauty #FragmentsOfGood

A Song

Sometimes you like a song so much that you can't stop listening to it. Ever.

And then at some point of time,
your brain can't take any more of it so you start
avoiding the song; the song that, by then, [has]
broken your heart a million times.

The fact that you avoid it does not mean that
you love it any less but you feel like exploring
other music.

As you listen to all these other songs, you
sometimes realise that no sound that reaches your
ears will ever be as beautiful and heart breaking
and perfect and amazing and painful as that song
was.

And then, one day, you'll hear a different version
of that song, and smile as the memories of an
older time come rushing back to you, the
nostalgia smacking you in the face, and you fall in
love all over again, only to have your heart broken
a million times again.

Nov 25, 2021

Parents' Note: Shrey possessed a refined taste in music, listening to many different genres. He experimented also with instruments such as the synthesizer, harmonium, and guitar and a bit of vocals too, though he didn't stick to or excel in any of them. These musings were written in reference to the song "The Good Side" by Troye Sivan.

A Second Chance

I wake up. There are lights everywhere; blinding me. I flinch. It takes me a while to adjust to my surroundings.

In front of me, I can see a man dressed in rags, with ratty hair and rotten teeth. He doesn't quite look human. I blink for a second and realise the man has vanished.

"You're dead", I hear someone say.

I look for that someone; the source of the sound. "You can't see me; not in this form anyway", he says.

I ask him who he is and all he says back in response is, "I am."

The realisation that I'm talking to God suddenly hits me. I bow to no one in particular and ask how I can serve him.

He just says, "The same as last time; what was it like; being human?"

"Oh, it was much like drowning in a lake whilst dying of thirst.

Like Pandora, desperately holding on to hope;
The hope of better days to come.
Like a bird without a nest;
One keeps flying without rest or a destination in mind.
A bit like the flow of a river,
Gradually adding on to something bigger than itself.

It wasn't the best existence, but it was perfect nevertheless."

I can hear Him chuckle to Himself.

He says; "Would you like to take my place for a lifetime? In all my life, I have never gotten an answer quite like that. I'd like to be on the stage itself and not a spectator for one."

"I'm afraid I can't, my Lord. To be human and to be Him are worlds apart. If I allow you to be human, You shouldn't give me something lesser in value"

"What do you want then, human?" He asks?

I smile and say, "A second chance."

Jan 12, 2022
#Humanity #Handwritten #God #GodWishesToBeHuman #Quotes #WhatItMeansToBeHuman #BeingHuman #Books&libraries #Art

Parents' Note: These verses appear to us as Shrey's account of the moments immediately following his passing, where he negotiates and obtains for himself a re-incarnation, a second chance at life. The piece unfolds with Shrey awakening in an otherworldly realm and engaging in a direct conversation with God. As he candidly reflects on the complexities of human existence ('It wasn't the best existence, but it was perfect nevertheless'), Shrey declines an extraordinary offer from God to switch roles and become God himself. Instead, he expresses a heartfelt desire for a second chance at life, highlighting the profound beauty he finds in the imperfect yet perfect nature of being human.

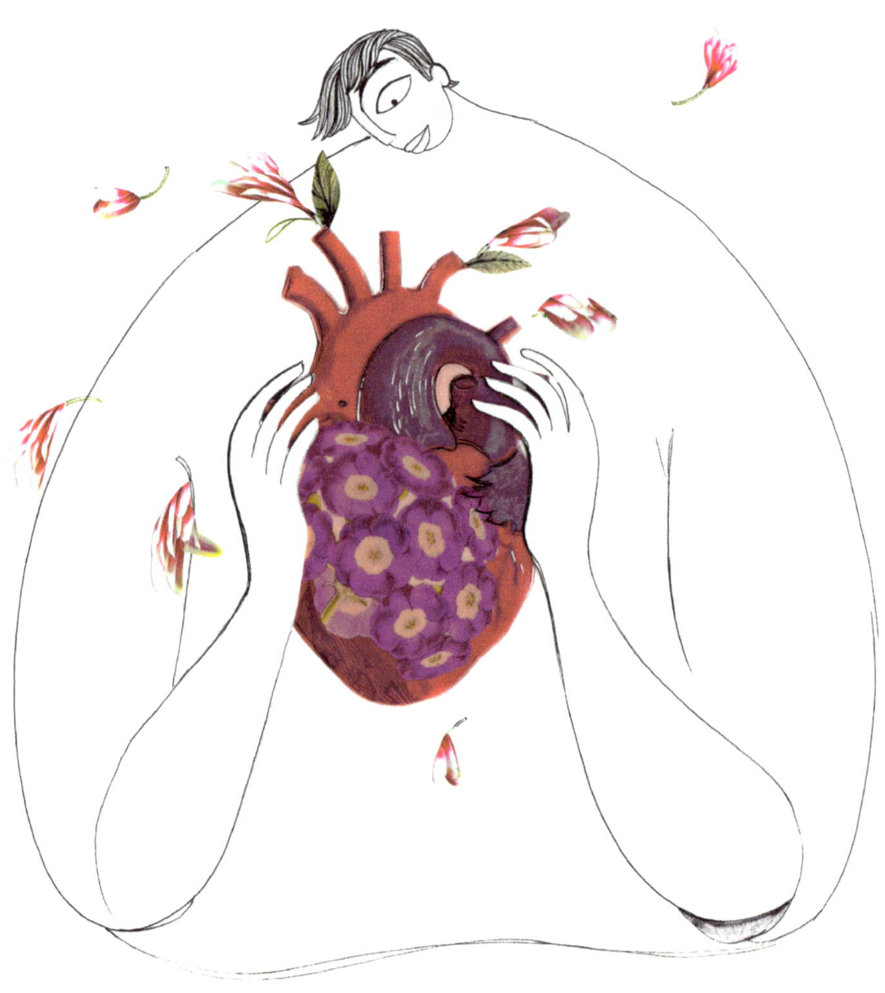

Fragrance

The shambles of a breaking heart
Held a wilting flower once.

Held it as it withered away,
Held its silver dust.

Clutched tightly in his fist,
Its fragrance still escaped.

Let out one last time,
Singing the sweet little song,
Of the autumn next.

May 25, 2022

Parents' Note: This is Shrey's final piece, left without a title. Little did he know
it would be his swansong. Son, we'll meet you someday, somewhere. Till then,
Godspeed, our lonely angel.

Epilogue

Ice-Cream delights

Shrey, Raga & Aslan

Someday, Somewhere

Son,

I know not the big picture
I know not the great scheme of things
I know not the secrets of life and death
I am but a mere mortal, a speck of dust.

What I know
Is only one thing
That I feel in my being
That I miss you, my son.

The stories, the theories of eternal soul
All sugar coatings, maybe?
How I like to believe in them still.
That I will see you again, one day
That I will hear your voice
Feel your touch, caress your lustrous hair
Feel your head on my arms
When you lie next to me
Hug you just once more.

False hopes, maybe these are
But hopes all the same
How I would love to cling on to them, my son.
My precious, precious son.

Did I value you less
When you were with me?
Can I compensate for all the times lost?

Someday, somewhere
Can we have more of the good times we had together?
They were a lot, but never enough, my son.

So, can we make a contract ?
Like we sometimes did, in jest.

Someday, somewhere
We will meet up
And complete the poetry of life we were making,
From which you had to leave in between.

My son, someday, somewhere...

Dad
July 2022

Much Gratitude

To those who crossed paths with Shrey in his short life,
Shaping him to be the fine man he was.

To those who stood with the family in the journey of grief,
When the curtains fell so abruptly, causing hearts to heave.

To Shrey's enduring spirit, vibrant, ever present,
Guiding us steadfastly through every challenge.

"
Meaning isn't in big perfect things
like the Moon or the Sun,
it is in the small imperfections
like the way the wind blows on a
cold day or the way flowers wither
in Autumn.

We don't live in a perfect world,
and that is precisely what
makes it perfect.